Big-Game Hunting
Bears, Elk, and Other Large Animals

Sloan MacRae

Open Season

PowerKiDS
press.
New York

To Bella. . . in case you decide to be a tomboy

Published in 2011 by The Rosen Publishing Group, Inc.
29 East 21st Street, New York, NY 10010

First Edition

Editor: Amelie von Zumbusch
Book Design: Greg Tucker
Photo Researcher: Jessica Gerweck

Photo Credits: Cover © www.iStockphoto.com/JurgaR; p. 4 Thinkstock/Getty Images; p. 5 Popperfoto/Getty Images; pp. 6, 7, 9, 14, 15, 17, 18–19, 21, 24–25, 26, 27 Shutterstock.com; p. 8 SuperStock/Getty Images; pp. 10–11 Ken James/Bloomberg via Getty Images; pp. 12, 16 © www.iStockphoto.com/Jason Lugo; p. 13 © www. iStockphoto.com/Ryan Howe; p. 20 Paul Nicklen/Getty Images; p. 22 Topher Donahue/ Getty Images; p. 23 © www.iStockphoto.com/Paul Tessier; p. 28–29 Tyler Stableford/ Getty Images.

Library of Congress Cataloging-in-Publication Data

MacRae, Sloan.
  Big-game hunting : bears, elk, and other large animals / Sloan MacRae. — 1st ed.
      p. cm. — (Open season)
  Includes index.
  ISBN 978-1-4488-0705-5 (library binding) — ISBN 978-1-4488-1371-1 (pbk.) —
ISBN 978-1-4488-1372-8 (6-pack)
  1. Big game hunting—Juvenile literature. I. Title.
  SK35.5.M236 2011
  799.2'6—dc22
                                    2010005272

Manufactured in the United States of America

CPSIA Compliance Information: Batch #WS10PK: For Further Information contact Rosen Publishing, New York, New York at 1-800-237-9932

Contents

Have you ever seen a bearskin rug? How about a stuffed moose head with giant antlers? These are the **trophies** of big-game hunters. People have been hunting big game for thousands of years. In the past, humans depended upon big-game hunting for **survival**. Successful big-game hunting can still mean the difference between life and death in some parts of the world. A single animal can

Big-game hunters, such as this father and daughter, like the challenge of hunting large, powerful animals.

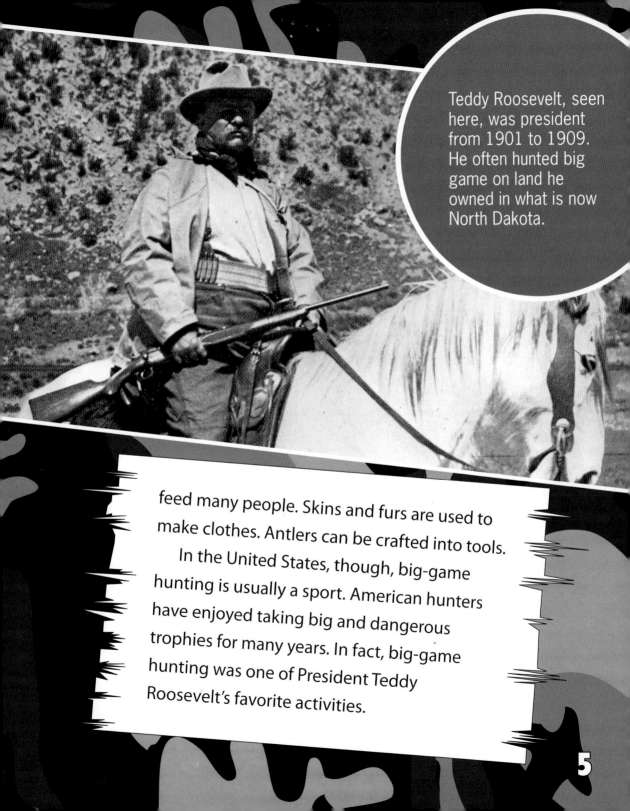

Teddy Roosevelt, seen here, was president from 1901 to 1909. He often hunted big game on land he owned in what is now North Dakota.

feed many people. Skins and furs are used to make clothes. Antlers can be crafted into tools.

In the United States, though, big-game hunting is usually a sport. American hunters have enjoyed taking big and dangerous trophies for many years. In fact, big-game hunting was one of President Teddy Roosevelt's favorite activities.

So What's the Big Deal?

Which animals are considered big game? You guessed it, big ones! Different states have different hunting laws, though, and some states differ on which animals they **classify** as big game. Bears, moose, and elk are all almost always considered big game. Some states, such as Alaska, permit the hunting of wolves. In Florida, you can hunt alligators!

Grizzly bears, such as this one, can be hunted in Alaska. It is illegal to hunt them in many other states, though.

6

This big-game animal is a moose. Moose are the largest members of the deer family. They live in northern North America, Europe, and Asia.

While big game is found across North America, certain animals are more common in particular areas. Black bears are hunted in states such as Pennsylvania and Montana. Elk can be found in Colorado and Wyoming, and moose are hunted in Maine and Alaska. You can find out which kinds of big game are hunted in your home state by going to the state's Web site.

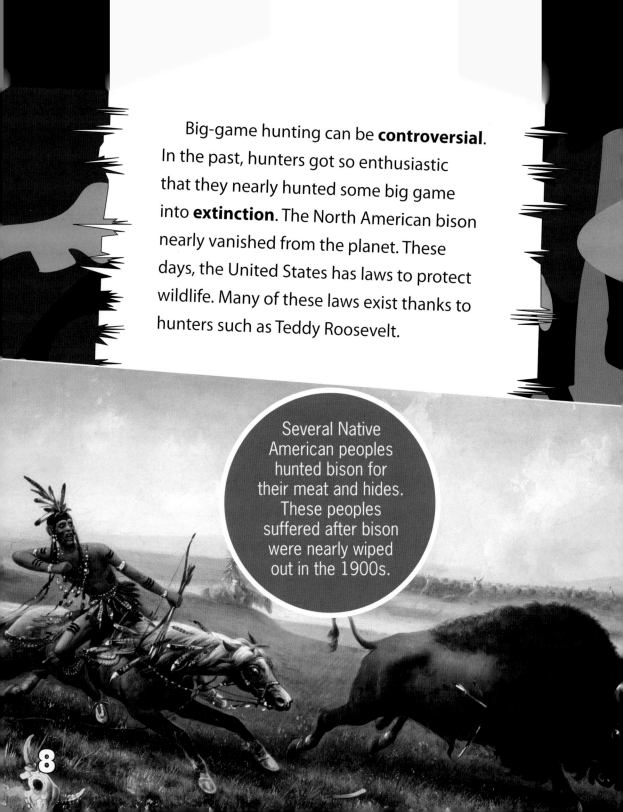

Big-game hunting can be **controversial**. In the past, hunters got so enthusiastic that they nearly hunted some big game into **extinction**. The North American bison nearly vanished from the planet. These days, the United States has laws to protect wildlife. Many of these laws exist thanks to hunters such as Teddy Roosevelt.

Several Native American peoples hunted bison for their meat and hides. These peoples suffered after bison were nearly wiped out in the 1900s.

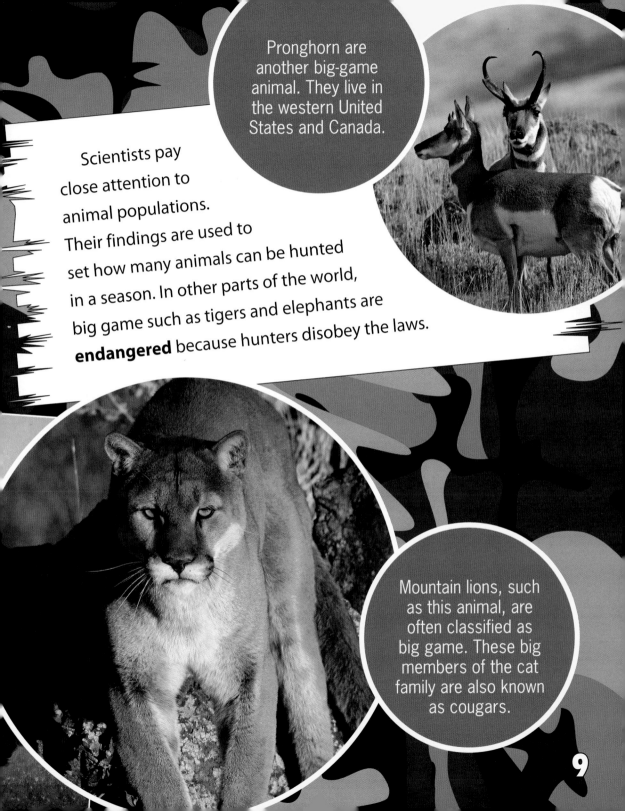

Pronghorn are another big-game animal. They live in the western United States and Canada.

Scientists pay close attention to animal populations. Their findings are used to set how many animals can be hunted in a season. In other parts of the world, big game such as tigers and elephants are **endangered** because hunters disobey the laws.

Mountain lions, such as this animal, are often classified as big game. These big members of the cat family are also known as cougars.

Bear Necessities

Do you want to hunt big game? First you will need to complete a hunting safety course. Your local sporting and outdoors clubs might offer one. The course will teach you important lessons about firearm safety.

Once you complete the course, it is time to get your hunting **license**. Just as a driver's license states that you can **legally** drive, a hunting license identifies you as a legal hunter in your state. The legal hunting age is usually 12, but laws vary from state to state. You will need to hunt with a parent or a guardian, and that person must also have a hunting license.

These men work for the California Department of Fish and Game. This is the group that gives out hunting licenses in California.

Unlike other licenses, you do not put your hunting license in your wallet. You pin it to the back of your jacket or coat. You can learn more about getting a hunting license from your state's Web site.

You will want to dress warmly because the seasons for hunting big game such as elk and moose are usually during the chilly part of the year. It is important to wear layers. Start with long underwear. Bring gloves that allow your fingers to move. Many states

This big-game hunter's orange hat and shirt make it easy for other hunters to notice him.

Hunting Facts

You might want to bring snacks and a lunch with you on your hunt. Avoid foods that make noise when you open or unwrap them.

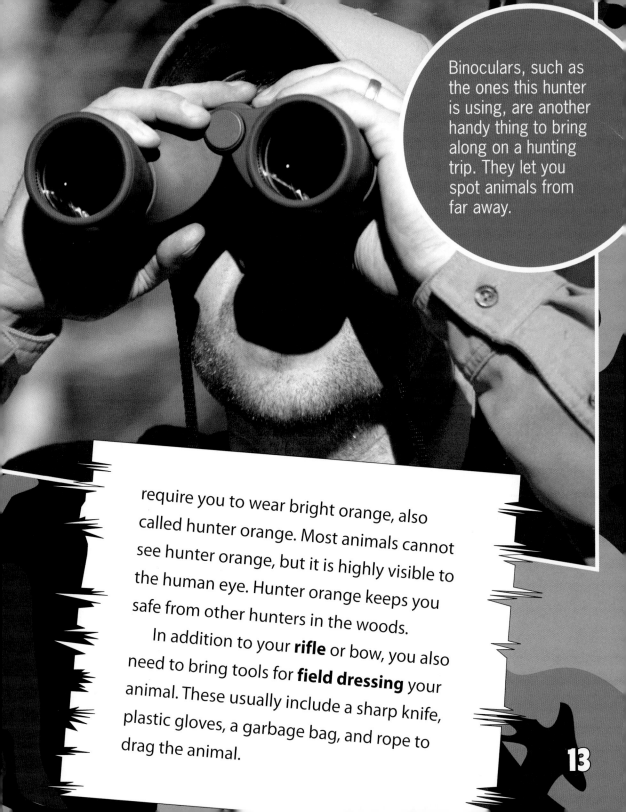

Binoculars, such as the ones this hunter is using, are another handy thing to bring along on a hunting trip. They let you spot animals from far away.

require you to wear bright orange, also called hunter orange. Most animals cannot see hunter orange, but it is highly visible to the human eye. Hunter orange keeps you safe from other hunters in the woods.

In addition to your **rifle** or bow, you also need to bring tools for **field dressing** your animal. These usually include a sharp knife, plastic gloves, a garbage bag, and rope to drag the animal.

Big Caliber

Big-game hunting requires different firearms from those used in other forms of hunting. You would not want to hunt black bears with the same gun you use for ducks! It is important to bring a big-**caliber** rifle and the correct **ammunition**.

Many big-game hunters use rifles, such as the one this man is holding. A rifle is a kind of long gun that is fired from the shoulder.

Hunting Facts

You can learn how to use firearms safely from the Web sites of organizations such as 4-H, the Boy Scouts of America, and the National Rifle Association.

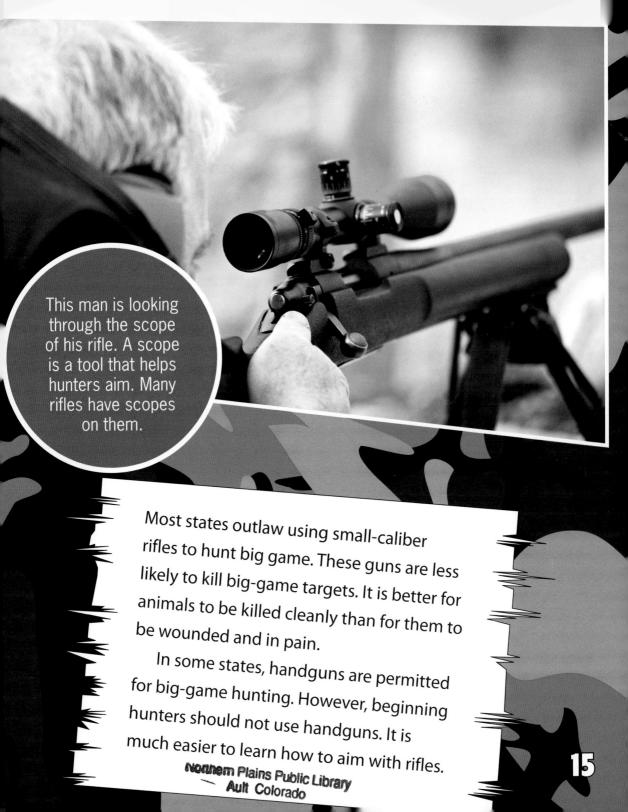

This man is looking through the scope of his rifle. A scope is a tool that helps hunters aim. Many rifles have scopes on them.

Most states outlaw using small-caliber rifles to hunt big game. These guns are less likely to kill big-game targets. It is better for animals to be killed cleanly than for them to be wounded and in pain.

In some states, handguns are permitted for big-game hunting. However, beginning hunters should not use handguns. It is much easier to learn how to aim with rifles.

15

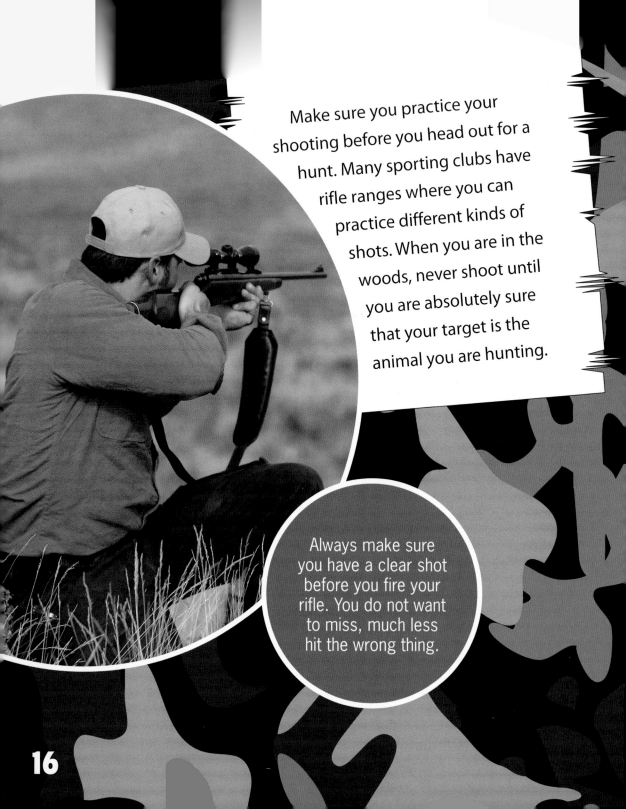

Make sure you practice your shooting before you head out for a hunt. Many sporting clubs have rifle ranges where you can practice different kinds of shots. When you are in the woods, never shoot until you are absolutely sure that your target is the animal you are hunting.

Always make sure you have a clear shot before you fire your rifle. You do not want to miss, much less hit the wrong thing.

Big Arrows

Hunting big game is challenging, but some hunters prefer an even greater challenge. They like to hunt with bows. Bow hunting is harder than hunting with a rifle because you have to get much closer to the animal. This means you must hunt silently. Your shot has to count. If a hunter misses with a rifle, there might be time for a

This big-game hunter has drawn his bow. He is now in position to shoot the arrow.

second shot. There will definitely not be time for a second shot with a bow because it takes longer to nock and aim an arrow.

In the United States, the most common hunting bow is the compound bow. This bow uses cables and pulleys. Some states also permit crossbow hunting. A crossbow looks like a combination between a bow and a gun. It has a trigger and is more powerful than a standard bow.

Bow hunters must be good trackers. It is rare for an arrow to kill big game instantly. Most animals will run away.

This man is using a crossbow. Crossbows are legal in some states, such as Alabama. In other states, such as Utah, they can be used only by disabled hunters.

It may take them a while to die. Bow hunters must follow an animal's trail. Some hunters have tracked their kills for several miles (km).

The most successful hunters know how to keep their eyes and ears open. Most big game are hard to see because their coloring blends in with the surroundings. Antlers often look like branches.

This moose's brown coat and antlers make it blend in with its surroundings. This method of hiding is known as camouflage.

Hunting Facts

It is hard to concentrate on hunting if you are lost. Get to know an area by going on walks before you go hunting there.

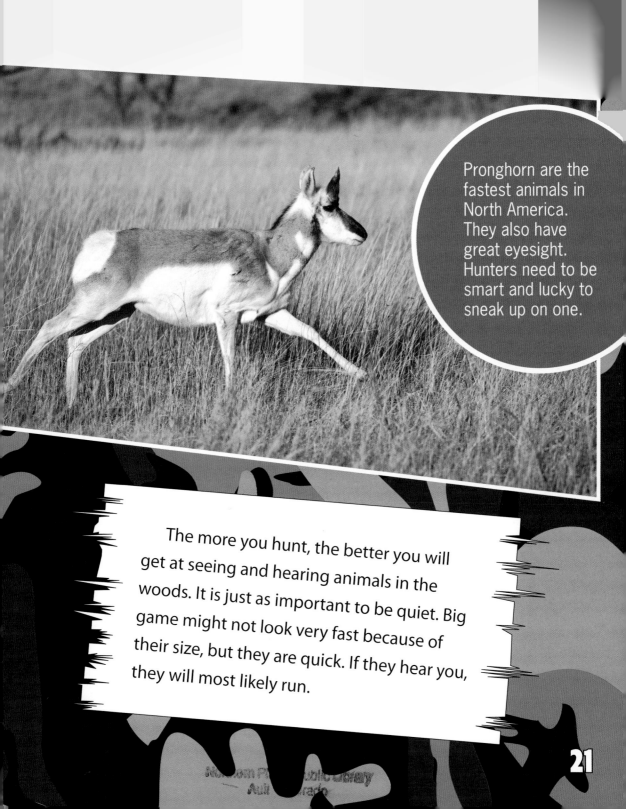

Pronghorn are the fastest animals in North America. They also have great eyesight. Hunters need to be smart and lucky to sneak up on one.

The more you hunt, the better you will get at seeing and hearing animals in the woods. It is just as important to be quiet. Big game might not look very fast because of their size, but they are quick. If they hear you, they will most likely run.

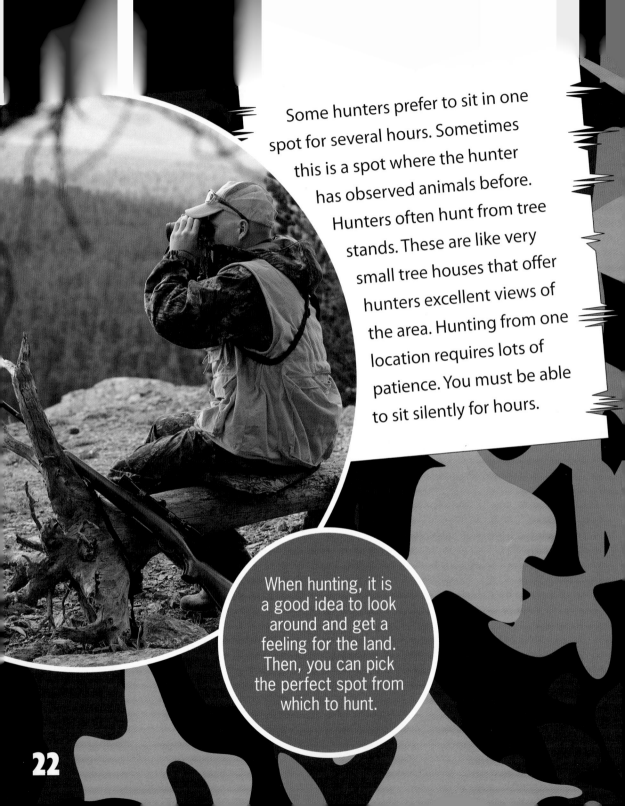

Some hunters prefer to sit in one spot for several hours. Sometimes this is a spot where the hunter has observed animals before. Hunters often hunt from tree stands. These are like very small tree houses that offer hunters excellent views of the area. Hunting from one location requires lots of patience. You must be able to sit silently for hours.

When hunting, it is a good idea to look around and get a feeling for the land. Then, you can pick the perfect spot from which to hunt.

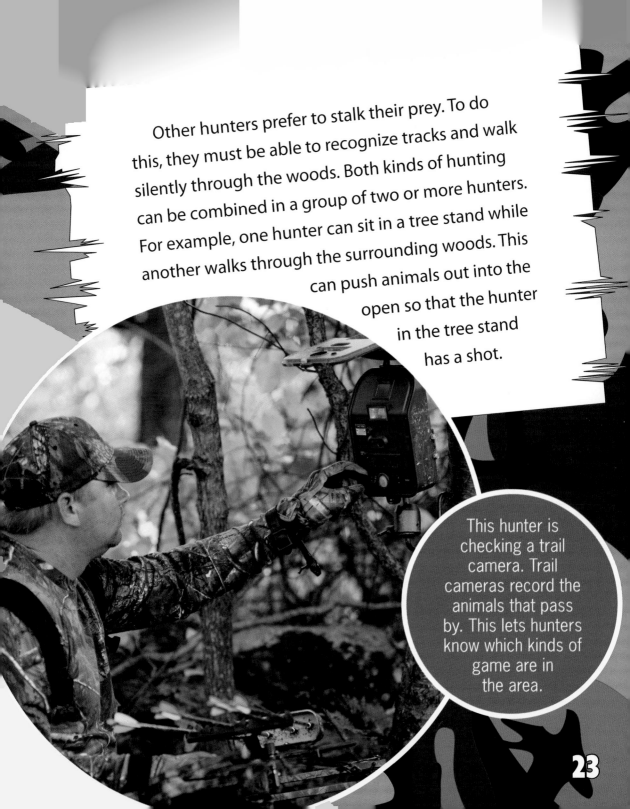

Other hunters prefer to stalk their prey. To do this, they must be able to recognize tracks and walk silently through the woods. Both kinds of hunting can be combined in a group of two or more hunters. For example, one hunter can sit in a tree stand while another walks through the surrounding woods. This can push animals out into the open so that the hunter in the tree stand has a shot.

This hunter is checking a trail camera. Trail cameras record the animals that pass by. This lets hunters know which kinds of game are in the area.

After the Kill

Congratulations! You shot a big-game animal. Now comes one of the most important parts of hunting. You must field dress your animal. Field dressing is also called cleaning. You must do this immediately because it prevents the meat from spoiling. You should get an adult to help you.

You also need to tag your animal. The tag is usually found on your hunting license. It is a form that you fill out and pin to your animal. You must supply details like the date and time of day so that your state's wildlife **agency** can record how many animals have been killed.

This young hunter shot a pronghorn in Wyoming. Hunters often have their picture taken after they make impressive kills like this one.

Enjoying the meat is one of the most satisfying parts of hunting. You can also create trophies for your friends to admire. These can be a bearskin rug or antlers to hang on the wall.

Hunting Laws

Good hunters know and follow their states' hunting laws. They hunt only animals that are in season. A certain animal's season is the only time it can be hunted. When hunting elk or moose, make sure you see antlers before you shoot. It is usually illegal to kill females. Hunting laws protect animal populations. Breaking a hunting law can mean an expensive fine or even the loss of your license. Breaking hunting laws on purpose is called

This bull, or male moose, is in Wyoming. There, moose can be hunted between September and November, depending on the part of the state they are in.

The moose here are a female (right) and her calf (left). Most hunters frown upon hunting big-game animals with babies. It is almost always against the law.

poaching. Examples of poaching include hunting animals out of season and killing more than your limit. Good hunters do not respect poachers because they are not hunting fairly. Hunting is a sport, after all. It is important that the animal gets a sporting chance.

Hunters Love Nature, Too

Hunting remains a controversial activity. Many people are simply not comfortable with the fact that animals are killed for sport. However, good hunters do not kill lightly. They respect wildlife. Many hunters are **environmentalists**. It is important for them to protect forests and wild places.

Big-game hunting is a skill that takes a lifetime to master. The only way to learn is by doing. It has been a part of North American history for thousands of years. Native Americans hunted bears and elk. Pioneers and cowboys

This man is big-game hunting on Colorado's Mount Sopris. Big-game hunting gives hunters the chance to spend time in many beautiful spots, such as this one.

did, too. Hunting provides people with a chance to reconnect with the natural world and with the past. It will remain a popular sport as long as people enjoy being challenged by nature.

Happy Hunting

- ⊕ Never shoot unless you are absolutely sure what your target is.

- ⊕ Most animals have much sharper hearing than you do, so be quiet!

- ⊕ Learn how to use a compass, and bring it with you.

- ⊕ Remember to clean your gun. This will protect it from rust and keep it firing cleanly.

- ⊕ You can purchase elk sprays and other scents that mask your human smell. These might smell bad to you, but you smell bad to animals.

- ⊕ Remember to bring warm clothing, especially if you are going to be sitting still for long periods of time. The first things to get cold are usually your fingers and your toes, so good gloves and thick socks are important.

- ⊕ If you hear shots from close by, pay attention. This could mean that a hunter missed. A scared and confused animal could be heading your way.

- ⊕ Remember to read all your state's hunting laws before you hit the woods.

- ⊕ Always make sure you have permission to hunt in a given area.

- ⊕ Be patient!

Glossary

agency (AY-jen-see) A special department of the government.

ammunition (am-yuh-NIH-shun) Things fired from weapons, such as bullets.

caliber (KA-luh-ber) Having to do with how wide a gun's opening is.

classify (KLA-seh-fy) To arrange in groups.

controversial (kon-truh-VUR-shul) Causing disagreement.

endangered (in-DAYN-jerd) In danger of no longer existing.

environmentalists (in-vy-run-MEN-tuh-lusts) People who want to keep the natural world safe.

extinction (ik-STINGK-shun) The state of no longer existing.

field dressing (FEELD DREH-sing) Removing the parts from a kill that would make the meat go bad.

legally (LEE-guh-lee) Done in a way that is allowed by the law.

license (LY-suns) Official permission to do something.

rifle (RY-ful) A long gun that is fired from the shoulder.

survival (sur-VY-val) Staying alive.

trophies (TROH-feez) Animal parts that hunters save to show others after a kill.

Index

Web Sites

Due to the changing nature of Internet links, PowerKids Press has developed an online list of Web sites related to the subject of this book. This site is updated regularly. Please use this link to access the list:
www.powerkidslinks.com/os/bgh/